The Ultimate Guide to

Anonymity

by Vincent J Davis

For additional information regarding the publisher or to get in

contact with the author, please visit:

https://otbtechh22f4wcuo.onion.ly/

Table of Contents

Introduction: Why Anonymity Matters

So, "why is anonymity so important," some of you may be asking. Anonymity is of importance for many reasons, but let's start with the fact that it is a basic human right. The Supreme Court of the United States of America has actually tied the right to be anonymous to the First Amendment right to free speech and association which reads, "Congress shall make no law respecting an establishment of religion, or prohibiting the free exercise thereof; or abridging the freedom of speech, or of the press; or the right of the people peaceably to assemble, and to petition the government for a redress of grievances." You have the right to speak freely which covers speaking anonymously, and freedom of the press means reporters are free to do so in anonymous fashion.

It is important to protect anonymity under the law as without such protection individuals who are working toward promoting social progress may face potential ramifications such as stalking, harassment, difficulty finding employment, and even threats against their life. Also, the right to privacy is guaranteed as a basic human right under international law. This is reflected in Article 12 of the Universal Declaration of Human Rights which states, "No one shall be subjected to arbitrary interference with his privacy, family, home or correspondence, nor to attacks upon his honour and reputation. Everyone has the right to the protection of the law against such interference or attacks." Without our right to be anonymous, social progress would stagnate and civilization as a whole would greatly suffer as a result.

The Five, Nine, and Fourteen Eyes

Now then, moving along onto the topic of mass surveillance: who's watching and how? Well, to put it simply, lots and lots of "eyes" are watching. While corporations do their fair share of tracking and logging users of electronic services and devices, the primary culprits are governments around the world. Naturally, a government would love to be able to have the ability to track and observe any and all citizens within (and even outside of) its jurisdiction for countless reasons. Is this starting to sound a bit like George Orwell's famous book "1984"? Well, that's good you are beginning to realize this because what we have in place today, and where we are rapidly headed in the future is very similar to that written about in Orwell's book. Oh, and did I forget to mention that most large corporations that participate in electronic surveillance cooperate and share the intelligence they collect with governments or does that simply go without saying?

Anyway, let's get you up to speed on who is watching what and how across the globe. We'll begin with what is most commonly referred to as "The Five Eyes." The Five Eyes is comprised of five countries that collaborate with one another in an effort to monitor each others citizens which allows them to circumvent established laws which would otherwise prevent them from conducting such surveillance on their own citizens. The Five Eyes (often abbreviated as FVEY) is comprised of the United States of America, Canada, New Zealand, Australia, and the United Kingdom. The basis of this signals intelligence co-op can be traced back to before WWII when Allied nations laid out their goals for how the world should look after the war was over. This then led to the creation of ECHELON (a surveillance program) which the Five Eyes claimed they would use to monitor citizens of the Eastern Bloc and the Soviet Union. In due time information was leaked indicating otherwise; that ECHELON was designed to monitor a far wider range of communications than just those originating or destined for the Soviet Union and/or the Eastern Bloc. As it would turn out, today it is public knowledge that ECHELON is (and according to investigations by Congress) always has been used to monitor a plethora of private communications. ECHELON was just the beginning, and today there have been and still are many many more mass surveillance programs in place.

Let's keep going, shall we? The Nine and Fourteen Eyes, as you can surmise, are groups of nine and fourteen countries with similar intelligence gathering and sharing agreements. The Nine and Fourteen Eyes are simply extensions of the Five Eyes. The Nine Eyes is composed of the Five Eyes plus Denmark, France, Netherlands, and Norway. The Fourteen Eyes is composed of the Nine Eyes plus Germany, Belgium, Sweden, Spain, and Italy. Keep these countries in mind as, in order to ensure our total anonymity and privacy, we must work to avoid passing our communications through these territories. Or, if we are within these territories or must pass communications through them, we must ensure that we utilize the highest level of encryption possible to make difficult the task of intercepting our communications. At this time decryption without the appropriate key is exceptionally difficult, but in the not so distant future such decryption may be much easier for adversaries once Quantum Computing is fully developed. Thus, as you can imagine, any communication that passes through these countries is at risk of being stored for future decryption. Case and point: the NSA's Utah Data Center. While its purpose is "classified," it doesn't take a rocket scientist to figure out why they need the ability to store amounts of data that are on the order of exabytes or greater. But, let's stick to the basics for now, I will provide resources for you to learn more about what the Post-Quantum world will look like later on in this guide.

Operating System Selection

Operating system selection is arguably the most important part of any secure and/or anonymous operation. What many people fail to realize is that Windows and Macintosh are not privacy focused whatsoever. As a matter of fact, the latest version of Windows at the time this was written (Windows 10) reports user data to the Microsoft Corporation up to 5,000 times per day regardless of the user's chosen preferences. Needless to say, what Microsoft does with the user data they collect is anybody's guess despite what they claim to be doing with it. There's a reason I began the transition to Linux when I was a teenager; I'm nobody's fool.

And, if you yourself are still on the fence like I was when I first started waking up, that's okay. Let me go on and explain how Windows is the most vulnerable operating system in terms of viruses and malware. Yes, that Windows PC of yours (despite marketing tactics by Microsoft) is the most poor choice of operating system on the face of the planet in terms of security. There are many reasons for this such as how the Windows operating system was originally designed. But, in modern times, Windows has fixed many security flaws, and now it has a lot more to do with the fact that black hats specifically target Windows users because they tend to be the least tech savvy of all internet users. Also, Windows users are primarily targeted because Windows currently has the largest user base on the planet with most instances being found in residences where there is not the same level of protection as that which can be found within a large organization. Regardless of whether or not you have an anti-virus you put your privacy at risk by using Windows, and in my eBook on computer hacking I have elaborated a lot more on the matter. But, for now, let's leave it at this: Even when up against a Windows PC with the most up to date anti-virus software, it would be easy to infect a Windows user without the individual being aware it has even occurred should a black hat so desire.

Worried about all the programs that you won't be able to use because they aren't compatible with Linux? That's okay too! For starters, there are many different programs that function similarly to those native to Windows and MacOS. Also, as you will read later in this guide, I will teach you how to set up software (Virtualization Software) that will allow you to use any program you desire regardless of the operating system for which it was intended. That's the beauty of switching to Linux, you have absolutely nothing to lose and everything to gain!

For the remainder of this guide, the information covered will be geared toward users of the Linux operating system as Windows and Mac OS should be treated as insecure (and thus are not to be used by those who seek to become and remain anonymous.)

Password Selection

Password selection is of utmost importance when it comes to protecting your data both online and in person. I would imagine that you are pretty familiar with this concept, but how much do you know about how passwords are stored and how they can be cracked? If you thought to yourself, "not very," don't feel bad. Most people are clueless. By keeping people in the dark about such things, that's just one more way hackers, corporations, and/or governments are able to gain access to your private life should they so desire. Again, once Quantum Computing comes to fruition, the game is going to change DRASTICALLY regarding password selection so let me teach you some of the best practices for password selection today so you will be more than prepared for tomorrow.

Without delving into concepts such as MD5, PBKDF2, Scrypt, Argon2, and salt which will only further confuse you at this point in the learning process I will keep things extremely simple. Obviously, you know to chose a password that is not easily guessable. But, what's even better yet is choosing a password that is entirely random. This can be accomplished using a fancy piece of software that is known as "diceware." This software can be downloaded through the Debian packages repository once you have installed Linux. What it will do for you is generate a memorable password composed of random words.

As of present, a password 5-6 words in length (chosen by using diceware) should suffice. However, I would not recommend such a short password as technology advances extremely fast. I will tell you this though: until Quantum Computing becomes affordable, it should be safe to use a password between 7-10 words in length (again, chosen using diceware.) The words should be separated by spaces, else-wise the difficulty level goes down quite a bit. Such passwords will be safe to use until Quantum Computing comes about, after this point in time it is advised to increase password length to 15 words or more (one last time: chosen using diceware) or else an adversary could easily gain unauthorized access to your data if equipped with appropriate resources. Additionally, should you even so much as suspect the password to be compromised it is advised that you immediately change it.

Full Disk Encryption

Understanding and utilizing Full Disk Encryption is paramount to secure your "base" if you will. By utilizing full disk encryption one can be certain that no one will be able to hack into your computer even if they gain physical access. The methods in this particular guide should suffice for domestic use, but should one decide to travel abroad with their laptop or computer then consider creating a Hidden OS using Veracrypt as is discussed later in this guide. While it may not be fool-proof to do so, it greatly decreases your chances of having the data on the hidden OS scrutinized by an investigating party if you happen to be destined for a location where people are granted less freedom than in your home country. Doing so is important as privacy laws vary depending on jurisdiction, and some jurisdictions require the revealing of encryption keys to authorities upon request. Thus, by using Veracrypt to create a hidden OS, you can potentially avoid having the entire contents of your hard drive exposed while still providing a key to decrypt the Decoy Operating System. As always though, speak with an attorney if you are uncertain about the laws in the jurisdiction to which you will be traveling.

With no further delay though, let me tell you all about LUKS! LUKS is an acronym for Linux Unified Key Setup. LUKS is very simple to use and set up, just make sure you utilize diceware to select a secure password. By using LUKS your entire hard drive will be encrypted and even if someone manages to steal or make a copy of the hard drive, provided you use a strong enough password, there is nearly zero chance of them being able to access your data. Just make sure not to lose the password for LUKS because there is no way to recover the data if you do. I've personally lost my LUKS password before and using every trick in the book I was unable to hack into my own computer!

LUKS can also be downloaded and set up on other Linux distributions should you so desire, but I will not offer much coverage on this topic here due to the level of technicality involved. All necessary files and information for set up on other distributions of Linux outside of Linux Mint can readily be found here: https://gitlab.com/cryptsetup/cryptsetup

Browser Selection

Browser selection is another very important thing to consider when it comes to becoming and remaining anonymous while using the world wide web. Not all browsers were created equally, and some are definitely more secure than others. My personal preference is Firefox due to the fact that it is open source with lots of community support and it is easily customized. There are only a few other browsers that I can recommend due to their being open sourced and/or privacy-centric such as Chromium, Brave, and the Tor Browser Bundle (which makes use of the Tor Network which I will discuss more in depth in the section devoted entirely to the topic.) Each of these browsers have their pros and cons which I will briefly discuss below.

Chromium: A spin-off of Google's Chrome browser. It is open-source and does not subject its users to the same data collection practices as the Google Chrome browser making it a more privacy-centric alternative. Keep in mind that if you do choose to use this safer browsing alternative that you must keep up on updating it manually as it does not allow automatic updates. Keeping Chromium up to date is important as out of date versions are more likely to have security vulnerabilities that will quickly become known to potential hackers. This is true of any software you use, not just Chromium/web browsers of course. Also, there is no way to block WebRTC in the browser itself. So, in order to prevent WebRTC leaks in Chromium it is ideal to download a trusted add-on.

WebRTC is something that I was going to devote an entire section of this guide to, but decided it should suffice to mention it as I discussed other topics such as browsers and VPNs. WebRTC (aka Web Real Time Communication) allows website to make direct connections with you which in turn can leak your real IP even if you use a VPN. It is ideal to block WebRTC via browser settings or via a trusted browser add-on if your end goal is anonymity online no matter the browser you use.

In conclusion, Chromium is a good alternative to what I consider the golden standard: Firefox. That is, provided you are willing to take the extra steps required to keep it up to date and secure.

Brave: Brave is a nifty browser based on Chromium that deserves recognition for the simple fact that it is more mainstream and intends to make users aware of privacy and security flaws that are present in other browsers. Brave, while claiming to be more private and secure, is only marginally improved compared to the level of safety that can be gained by using the user.js file mentioned in the "Firefox Browser Privacy Modifications" section of this guide along with appropriate privacy related add-ons. Brave is definitely a step above the rest by offering ad blocking and tracker blocking, Tor integration with private browsing, and even blockchain based token payments to content creators as a reward system.

So, while there is a lot of improvement in security over almost all other browsers, there is still room for improvement which will be covered in the next few sections. Brave ranks slightly above Firefox out of the box in terms of security and privacy, however with some modifications Firefox is far superior.

Tor Browser: Tor Browser is essentially just a portable version of Firefox with some minor modifications to allow for all users to appear very similar to one another. Tor browser routes all traffic through the Tor Network meaning using it to browse the web makes you relatively anonymous. Obviously, there is a lot more that goes into becoming anonymous than just using Tor Browser, but it is definitely a good browser if you want some basic protection. The downfall is that your traffic can be intercepted by rogue Tor Nodes if it is encrypted. And, other traffic analysis is possible to figure out your identity if an adversary so desired. Plus, without a VPN (or at very least a Tor Bridge) it would be known to your ISP that you were using Tor. So, with the proper procedures in place, Tor Browser is definitely an improvement. But, Tor Browser is no replacement for a security hardened installation of Firefox.

Browser Fingerprint

Browser fingerprint can be thought of as your unique mark left as you visit a web page. Back in the early days of the internet, this used to be composed of simple things like your IP, browser type, and operating system. But, with many advances in technology having taken place there are countless other ways that you can be fingerprinted as you browser the world wide web. Every time you visit a website, this browser fingerprint is logged and recorded. This is what we must modify should we desire to become anonymous when using the internet. The number of things that can be used to identify you are constantly growing, but as of present the methods covered in this guide should be enough to effectively alter your browser fingerprint to the point it cannot be linked to you.

Keep in mind, when modifying your browser fingerprint your goal is to have your fingerprint look as close to the same as the largest user-base you can; there's safety in numbers. You want to appear the same as everyone else so as to not arouse suspicion that you are trying to hide. To see how similar your browser fingerprint is to the rest of the population, please visit:

https://panopticlick.eff.org

For even more resources for testing your browser so as to become aware of just what identifying information may be being sent to the websites you visit, please check out:

https://browserleaks.com/

Firefox Browser Privacy Modifications

Firefox is my favorite browser as it is tried and true; it is the golden standard by which I judge all other browsers. There are countless ways that one can modify their browser to increase security and privacy through the "about:config" settings in the browser, but without advanced knowledge of such things it is possible to do more harm than good. So, this section is dedicated to explaining some of the basic concepts and offering helpful pointers on where to find more information and pre-configured files that can be implemented to harden your Firefox installation.

I will start by saying that everyone's objectives are different. Your reason for wanting to become anonymous may vary from the next person's reason. However, the methods of becoming anonymous are all very similar. As I mentioned earlier, by altering the "about:config" settings in Firefox we can harden our browsers to become more secure thus increasing anonymity and privacy. A list of all possible security and privacy adjustments can be found at: http://kb.mozillazine.org/Category:Security_and_privacy-related_preferences (Unfortunately, this is not able to be viewed of SSL/TLS)

If you would like to configure your "about:config" settings to be as secure as possible you may opt to use a "user.js" file that provides you with all necessary "about:config" modifications. A "user.js" file is a file that functions as a template telling Firefox to permanently keep certain modifications in place. The file can be downloaded and saved to the user profile directory of your firefox installation. All necessary files and installation information for the "user.js" I use personally can be found here:

https://github.com/pyllyukko/user.js

Firefox Browser Privacy Add-Ons

There are many Firefox Browser privacy add-ons available, but I will only cover those that are beginner-friendly and worth mentioning in this guide. These add-ons go a step above what can be offered via "about:config" modifications, and some can even be used to spoof certain information sent to websites which further increases your anonymity.

1.) LessPass – LessPass is password generator and manager that functions to allow users the ability to keep track of their passwords across devices without the need for a password vault. LessPass is considered more secure than a password manager in the sense that none of the user's information is stored in any way. If there are certain password requirements such as special characters, capital letters, or numbers, LessPass allows the user to select these preferences. The password is generated based on the website, the username, and a master password. There is also a feature that allows you to increase security by changing the "counter" number which will allow you to generate a new password with the same information. For more information, check out: https://lesspass.com

2.) CanvasBlocker – Canvas Data is one method of browser fingerprinting that can be taken care of through "about:config" modifications. However, there exists an add-on that is known simply as "CanvasBlocker" which prevents such fingerprinting by either blocking or spoofing Canvas Data. More information can be found here:

https://addons.mozilla.org/en-US/firefox/addon/canvasblocker/

3.) Decentraleyes – Decentraleyes is useful by preventing Content Delivery Networks from delivering third-party content which compromises users' security. Decentraleyes instead intercepts such requests and delivers localized content. More information can be found here:

https://addons.mozilla.org/firefox/addon/decentraleyes/

4.) HTTPS Everywhere – Just as the name implies, HTTPS Everywhere prevents websites that do not offer SSL from being accessed by the user and it forces SSL versions of sites to be requested instead of insecure versions. This ensures that all data transmitted is encrypted which reduces the possibility that an adversary may gain information as to your browsing habits. This add-on is part of a collective effort between the Electronic Frontier Foundation and the Tor Project. More information can be found here: https://www.eff.org/https-everywhere

5.) NoScript Security Suite – This add-on offers excellent protection from potentially malicious javascript, java, and flash found on webpages. Javascript, java, and flash all have potential to expose a users private information or deliver malicious instruction to be run on the users computer. By using this add-on the user can chose what he or she wants to allow thus providing a huge increase in overall security. More information can be found here: https://addons.mozilla.org/firefox/addon/noscript/

6.) Privacy Badger – Privacy Badger takes your privacy seriously! This add-on blocks and prevents advertisers and third-party trackers from monitoring you across the web. It is not all encompassing however, thus it is suggested it be used in combination with another more extensive blocker such as uBlock

Origin. More information can be found here:

https://www.eff.org/privacybadger

7.) uBlock Origin – This is like Privacy Badger on steroids! uBlock Origin is capable of blocking far many more trackers and advertisements than any other ad blocker available. For more information please visit:

https://addons.mozilla.org/firefox/addon/ublock-origin/

8.) Spoof Timezone – Spoof Timezone is useful for users that wish to change the information submitted to websites about their local timezone. It is able to be customized which is good because the defaults transmit a timezone that looks suspect in my humble opinion. To change the transmitted information simple go to the add-on settings and modify as you desire. This add-on is exceptionally useful for those using a VPN or proxies since it makes it more believable that you are located where your IP indicates. For more information please visit:

https://addons.mozilla.org/en-US/firefox/addon/spoof-timezone/

9.) User-Agent Switcher and Manager – This add-on is great for spoofing information related to your user-agent. Your user-agent contains information about you browser, and your operating system. With this add-on it is possible to spoof such information as you see fit, and you can even set a specific user-agent for specific sites if you desire. The only downfall would be that this spoofing becomes suspect when javascript identifies your browser and operating system. Thus, it is recommended you use this is combination with the NoScripts Security Suite for maximal effectiveness. There are other similar add-ons available, but this one is the best of the bunch! More information can be found here: https://addons.mozilla.org/en-US/firefox/addon/user-agent-string-switcher/

VPNs

Virtual Private Networks are of immense usefulness to those who desire to be anonymous when using the world wide web. There are many different providers available, but not all of them are equal! Some VPN service providers log and monitor user data (specifically those available for free.) But, there are many with a no logs policy which can even be purchased anonymously by using cryptocurrency. As of present, the two best providers are NordVPN and ExpressVPN in my opinion.

NordVPN has actually had its no logs policy verified de facto when a subpoena was issued for information regarding a high profile murder case involving a politician. NordVPN advised the authorities that it was unfortunate that their services had been misused, but that they kept no logs and thus could not provide any relevant user data. These services do not permit the use of their servers for illegal activities, but they do no keep logs which ensures their users' privacy.

Both ExpressVPN and NordVPN are out of the jurisdiction of the Fourteen Eyes and thus can be considered safe from government surveillance. While these companies are based outside of the jurisdiction of the Fourteen Eyes, I highly recommend only using servers of theirs that are outside of the Fourteen Eyes as this further decreases the opportunity for your data to be intercepted as it passes through these jurisdictions which is still entirely possible.

Also, keep in mind that a VPN does not guarantee anonymity, it just makes it more difficult to positively identify an internet user. For maximum security it is advised to simultaneously use multiple methods of anonymization.

In terms of value, NordVPN is the best bang for your buck by offering 5200+ servers for one of the lowest rates out of all major VPN providers in business today. More information on pricing can be found here: https://join.nordvpn.com/order/?menu=pricing

Both VPN services (ExpressVPN and NordVPN) are able to be used in tandem with OpenVPN equipped routers (more on this topic later in the guide) which will allow you to route all of the devices in your home through the VPN while only using up one connection slot. ExpressVPN has a simultaneously connected device limit of only 3, while NordVPN offers you up to 8 simultaneous connection.

These are simply my personal favorites, but for more information on other VPN service providers feel free to check out one of my favorite websites for such: https://TheBestVpn.com/

Keep in mind it is always best to do more in depth research just as I did before deciding on what service provider to utilize. One example of a reason why is that some VPN providers may have servers located in one country while advertising them as another country due to where the IP address is linked. This means that you may be using a server that is physically located in Italy which is within the 14 Eyes, but yet the VPN provider may list it as an Estonian server (which is outside the Fourteen Eyes) if that's where its IP is registered for example.

TOR/I2P Network

The Tor Network is an amazing concept that was originally funded in large part by the US Government themselves believe it or not. This anonymity network is capable of routing your internet traffic through various nodes that are located across the world and run by volunteers to keep your identity from being discovered. There are however some pitfalls that can take place when using such a service.

One thing to keep in mind is that many governments operate Tor nodes in an attempt to monitor network traffic. This can allow governments the ability to discover a user's probable identity. Also, any traffic not destined for a site on the Tor Network itself or protected by SSL is easily intercepted and many times will contain enough data to identify a user. These are one of many reasons is why it is important to use a VPN with the Tor Network if you desire to remain anonymous online. More in-depth discussion on such topics will occur later in this guide.

The I2P Network, also known as the Invisible Internet Project Network, is an overlay network that routes traffic over the Tor Network in a manner known as "Garlic Routing." The way this works is that your data is sent through the network along with other users' data simultaneously, and as the data approaches its destination it veers off from the original chunk. All data is sent encrypted, and only websites on the I2P Network are accessible to users of the I2P Network. This makes the I2P Network more secure than the Tor network as such routing makes network data analysis extremely difficult, and there is no risk of exposure by visiting websites that are not secure. Additionally, it should be noted that the I2P Network is somewhat quicker than the Tor Network due to the fact that it uses Garlic Routing. However, the I2P Network has less of a user-base and of course the sites that can be visited through the I2P Network are limited as well.

Using I2P is very easy and it utilizes the same browser you use for day to day tasks. To find out more information about using the I2P Network, please visit: https://geti2p.net/en/

SOCKS5 Proxies

SOCKS5 Proxies can be thought of as simply servers that act as relays for internet traffic. SOCKS5 Proxies have differing levels of anonymity offered depending on how their owners have decided to set them up. The best SOCKS5 Proxies are known as "Elite SOCKS5 Proxies" and they work to anonymize all connections.

SOCKS5 Proxies are easy to set up since they work through your existing browser to function. All you have to do is obtain the proxy's IP address and the port number on which it is listening, then input the information in your browser's settings. Once everything is set up you will now be able to visit websites through the proxy which will make you appear to be surfing the web from whatever geolocation the IP address of the proxy is registered. In Firefox, simple go to Preferences, click on Network Settings, then select "Manual proxy configuration." You should know what to do from here.

"But wait, how do I find a SOCKS5 Proxy to use," you

might ask. This is an excellent question as there are many providers for SOCKS5 Proxies across the web. Not all providers are equal however. Many free providers exist, but their services are subpar. The best SOCKS5 Proxy providers allow for anonymous payment using cryptocurrency, have low latency and high uptime, provide fresh proxies on a regular basis, and offer offer private proxies. Selecting the right provider is key because many SOCKS5 Proxies are used for nefarious purposes and thus quickly become "blacklisted" by websites which makes it so that you cannot access these websites through said proxy. This is only an issue typically with shared proxy services, so a private SOCKS5 Proxy provider is ideal. These private proxy services will usually require some form of payment, and thus a provider should accept cryptocurrency to allow maximum anonymity of the user. Having high uptime and low latency is important to keeping your web browsing experience smooth as you surf the web, and having fresh proxies that are regularly updated is important so all of your activity doesn't get tied to a handful of IP addresses which would compromise your efforts to stay anonymous.

One of the more unique SOCKS5 Proxy providers that has a focus on providing anonymity to its users is ProxyRack, whose primary function is to serve rotating proxies to its user-base. ProxyRack provides rotating proxies that allow you to connect to one static IP which then routes your traffic through SOCKS5 Proxies that rotate as you browse the web to provide the highest level of anonymity available through their service. They also allow "sticky proxies" which allow you to use one specific SOCKS5 exit node for between 3-30 minutes before it changes. This can be useful depending on your objectives. Payment is offered through cryptocurrency. For more information please visit their website at: https://www.proxyrack.com/

Another exceptionally good SOCKS5 Proxy provider that functions in the more traditional manner is PremSocks. This site is excellent and trustworthy for obtaining fresh, live, and private SOCKS5 proxies. They accept payment via cryptocurrency to help ensure you remain anonymous. All of their proxies are "Elite SOCKS5 Proxies" which means they function completely anonymously. For more information please visit:

https://premsocks.com/

Keep in mind a SOCKS5 proxy is a very poor way to become anonymous while online and should be combined with other anonymity techniques. SOCKS5 proxies are however very useful if you wish to operate a proxy chain or if you desire an exit node in a specific geographical location for one reason or another. Much more detail on such things is found in the section of this guide titled "Proxy Chains."

Anonymous Search Engines

Search engines are our best friend as anyone who uses the internet will tell you. However, most of the mainstream search engines also track and log user data like no other! If you are not okay with your search history being logged and monitored by Google, then read on.

There are three specific search engine providers that I can recommend to you that will eliminate you having to be subjected to privacy-violating corporations.

The first, and best, is Startpage (aka IXQuick.) This search engine is fantastic and even encrypts the search terms usually found in the URL of other providers after you submit a query. This service is my absolute favorite for many reasons; you can even view the resulting search results anonymously through their proxy service! Based out of Europe and having been around since 2006 its no wonder they are in first place.

My second favorite is DuckDuckGo, they offer complete privacy and even have a .Onion website as well! There are two downfalls to this service though: the company is indeed US based, and the core is not open-source; keep this in mind if you decide to use their service. While they are very user-friendly, their service can easily be compromised since they are within the jurisdiction of the Five Eyes. Plus, the search engines core source code cannot be audited by third-parties meaning we do not have any idea as to how secure or private it actually may be. But, none the less, they are still my second favorite private search engine.

The last search engine I can suggest for anonymous web searches is SearX. It is considered a metasearch engine; it compiles search results from other search engines on the web for its users. They do not log user data, they present no ads, and they do not track either. Also, they have a .Onion website as well! I do not personally care for this search engine as much as the previous two, but then again they are totally open-source unlike DuckDuckGo. That being the case, there are numerous instances of the service operating by third parties all over the internet. A list of instances for your reference can be found here:

https://github.com/asciimoo/searx/wiki/Searx-instances

While there is not much to say about these services as they do exactly as they should, I at very least have ranked them in order of my most favorite to least and provided you with what I know about them in terms of what they have to offer in terms of privacy.

Bitcoin Anonymization Methods

So, you probably know a little bit about bitcoin being that you have purchased this guide. That's a start I suppose, but you have only just scratched the surface. Many people believe that bitcoin is a fully anonymous means of payment, but this could not be further from the truth. Bitcoin is actually one of the most public ways of sending funds to another party. All transactions are forever stored in the blockchain, and thus all of your business becomes public when you decide to use Bitcoin. But, there are ways to go about anonymizing your transactions.

Bitcoin can be purchased from many sources, but as of 2019 most sources will link your purchase of Bitcoin to your physical identity in some way. This puts people in a small conundrum if they wish to use Bitcoin anonymously to pay for goods and services. This is where Bitcoin mixing services come into play.

We've covered the best methods to anonymize your internet connection and how to secure your browser, but how then does one use these techniques to anonymize Bitcoins?

Its as easy as 1, 2, 3!

1.) Purchase Bitcoins and store them in your personal wallet; at this point it is quite obvious they are yours.

2.) Use Electrum Bitcoin Wallet through Tor to generate multiple receiving addresses

3.) Visit a bitcoin mixer such as "Bitcoin Mixer" (https://bitcoinmixer.eu/) using the anonymity techniques you learned previously (or, even better yet, read the guide through as even better methods of attaining anonymity will be discussed later) and use the addresses that were generated by Electrum for the outputs.

That's the gist of it anyway. The idea is to separate the coins from anything that could possibly link them to their original source. Using Electrum through Tor is ideal, but it is also advised that one should use a VPN prior to connecting to the Tor Network as well. At this point you should know enough to figure out the nitty gritty yourself though.

WARNING! There has recently been a situation in which

the world's largest bitcoin mixing service was taken offline due to abuse of its services by criminals. During the preceding months/year leading up to the servers being seized, authorities somehow managed to log certain interactions with the servers. This information is now to be thoroughly analyzed by the authorities governing the jurisdiction in which the service was located and the findings will be shared with foreign intelligence official upon completion. This is just a reminder that if you are thinking about using any information in this guide for unlawful activities, that you may find yourself on the wrong side of the law sooner than you think. This method of bitcoin anonymization does allow for plausible deniability, but it should never be used for criminal acts. The reason this section is included is to provide information on how to prevent a person or organization from gaining knowledge of your personal bitcoin address and subsequently studying your spending habits by monitoring your activity on the blockchain.

[See also the section titled "Monero, Dash, Verge, Bitcoin Dark and Zcash" for another method of anonymization. (Hint: Bitcoin →

Monero $\rightarrow$ Bitcoin using shapeshift = Bitcoins of untraceable origin.)]

Stylometrics

Stylometry, loosely define, is the application of the study of linguistic style. When using the internet your communications with other parties may be anonymous through the use of Pseudonyms and the aforementioned anonymization techniques, but your style of writing is something that can be used to identify you as well! It doesn't take much more than a few thousand words to positively identify the author of a literary work. This is part of the reason why I care not that my identity is publicly known as I sell this guide. Even if I were to anonymously provide such information, it would be relatively easy to identify the author of this work as me with the right tools.

My purpose for having made note of this in this document is to make people aware of the fact that stylometrics is an often overlooked thing when it comes to becoming anonymous. It is necessary that you change pretty much everything about the manner in which you write if you are to remain truly anonymous online. One recommended method is to mimic the writing style of another author. Fortunately, it is not difficult to defeat stylometric analysis and thus stylometric analysis as a sole means of positively identifying a party is extremely unreliable. None-the-less, keep this in mind as you proceed!

Printing, Scanning/Copying, and Pictures/Images

Did you realize that any time you send a picture using digital devices that there is metadata attached to it known as "EXIF data" which contains identifying information up to and often times including the latitude and longitude where the originating device was when the picture was taken?

No? Well, you are not alone! Most people do not realize that EXIF data even exists, let alone what all it can do to de-anonymize them. So, how do we prevent EXIF data from exposing our true identities when we desire to remain anonymous? Simple, use a tool that strips EXIF data prior to sending it over the web and you are as good as gold!

EXIF data stores information about the device used to take photographs such as manufacturer/model of the device, time and date the photo was taken, geographical location at the time the photo was taken, pixel resolution, the devices exact serial number and more. The NSA actually collects, stores, and analyzes EXIF data since it contains such valuable identifying information as a matter of fact!

To get rid of EXIF data is simple since the advent of applications designed specifically to remove it. One good app for removing EXIF data is "Photo Metadata Remover for Android." For iOS, you can download "Metapho," which can remove EXIF data if you pay for the in-app purchase required to do so. But, this is not the only way to get rid of EXIF data.

If you have access to a PC, you can get rid of EXIF data by using GIMP. Simply open your photograph in GIMP, go to File > Export As and make sure to export the photo as a jpg. Click Export then go to Advanced Options and uncheck the box that reads "Export EXIF data" then click Export to finish. That's it! Pretty simple right?

Moving on to remaining anonymous when printing things is another story entirely. Obviously, this falls somewhat outside of the realm of remaining anonymous online, but it should be noted that all LaserJet printers contain security features that result in invisible "tracking dots" that can be used to identify the exact printer from which the document originated. To get around this in modern times, I highly recommend printing only with an InkJet printer if you plan on printing documents that are politically charged or otherwise deemed offensive in some way. There can be serious ramifications depending on the situation if your identity is linked to certain political agendas/ideologies or other similarly controversial topics. This is where remaining anonymous when printing may come in handy.

For more information on "tracking dots," please visit: https://www.eff.org/issues/printers

Pretty Good Privacy (PGP)

PGP is an excellent method of encrypting communications normally done in plain text that are transmitted via the web such as through email. PGP is extremely easy to use and uses what is known as Asymmetric Cryptography or Public-Key Cryptography. The concept is simple, both parties have a public key and a private key. The public key of the receiving party contains information used by the sending party to encrypt the contents of the messages being sent to the receiving party. The receiving party is the only one that can read the messages once encrypted since he/she is the only one with the private key which is what is used to decrypt the messages. Public keys can be known by anyone since they can only encrypt messages, but cannot decrypt them. So long as the private keys remain safe, both parties can rest assured knowing their communications are secure.

There are many graphical user interfaces that can be used for PGP encryption on Linux; my personal favorite is GPA (Gnu

Privacy Assistant.) For more information regarding such programs,

please visit the GnuPG website at: https://GnuPG.org/

Communication Methods (Email, IM, Voice Chat/Phone Calls, Video Chat, etc.)

Communications over the web can be tricky if your goal is anonymity and security. Obviously, the use of pseudonyms and encryption such as PGP are paramount. However, there are other things that must be considered such as where your email server is located (and their privacy policies) and the ease of use of certain protocols. While PGP may be fine and dandy is cases where total anonymity and security is required, there are many cases where one may simply wish to have something more user-friendly at hand.

Email service providers vary greatly in the services they offer, but most mainstream providers have one thing in common: they don't care about the users privacy. Google, hotmail, yahoo, and the like are all garbage in my opinion. The best providers offer full end-to-end encryption and store emails securely away from prying eyes. Three providers that come to mind are Tutanota, Protonmail, and msgSafe.

Tutanota, based in Germany, offers end-to-end encryption between users and is free to use. They even offer you the ability to communicate securely with those who do not have a Tutanota account by establishing a password with the receiving party through a secure communication channel who can then use it to decrypt your messages sent through Tutanota. Germany has very strict privacy laws and so your data is not only encrypted, but is protected by law. They never require any personal information of yours for registration (not even a phone number.) They even strip any identifying information from emails such as IP addresses. Also, they have apps for Android and iPhone. For more information or to sign-up, please visit: https://Tutanota.com

Protonmail, based in Switzerland, is the best of the best in my opinion. While registering for the service was a delicate process (despite claims that it is easy to register for a free account) for me, I still find the service itself to be spectacular. They are based out of Switzerland which is world renowned for their strict privacy laws. There is one small thing that may concern some people, the company itself has strong ties to the United States. This has led many people to speculate as to whether or not they may be cooperating with the US Government to allow backdoor access into their services. Again, this is total speculation and is not likely to be the case, but it is noteworthy none-the-less. I have a firm belief that the company is very honest and up-front, but we also utilize many other service providers for communications to reduce our risks. Your mileage may vary with this one.

MsgSafe is a relatively unheard of contender that deserves some attention. This company is based in Panama (far outside the reach of the Fourteen Eyes,) and has technology support centers in Curaçao.

This provider offers end-to-end encrypted email services much the same as Tutanota and Protonmail do, but they do require you to link an outside email account upon registering. No big deal, simply use one created anonymously on Tutanota and you're set.

MsgSafe is owned by parent company TrustCor whose mission statement is actually very similar to that of my own company's mission statement; "TrustCor's vision is to provide state-of-the-art, simple to use, privacy enhancing products and services for businesses and individuals." As the founder of OTB Technologies, I'd have to say that this company seems to stand for everything that I do. I mean hell, the TrustCor website even reads, *"Protect your digital privacy from advertisers, cyber-criminals, businesses and governments!"* That's exactly what my company aims to help its clients do just the same! I'm going to have to give MsgSafe a thumbs up here since we are on the same wavelength despite the fact that they are largely overlooked as an email service provider. Oh, and while we are on the topic, it would appear that they have been working quietly to introduce end-to-end encrypted messaging services as well!

This leads me into the next topic of discussion, and one of my personal favorites: Instant Messaging. One such service that I mentioned previously is that offered by msgsafe, but as I also mentioned they are relatively unheard of and their app is very new. This means that not much has been done in terms of security audits. However, there are many other messaging platforms available at this time to choose from that offer end-to-end encryption. Each service with their own flavor if you will. I will offer a brief list of the most popular services available at this time.

Starting off I would like to make mention of Signal. Signal is excellent for messaging other users of the platform using encrypted communication protocols. Signal is extremely secure and even offers VoIP calling and video conferencing to other users of the platform. This platform is considered one of the most secure messaging services available in 2019. Unfortunately, its servers are in the United States meaning that it is within the jurisdiction of the Five Eyes. Also, it requires you to tie your actual identity to the program by syncing with your phone number and contacts (Though I suppose one could use a "burner phone" if desired.) It is available on both Android and iPhone as an app and it even offers a Desktop version for users of their mobile services to link their PCs with as well. For more information please visit their website at: https://signal.org/

Telegram is another extremely valuable tool that offers both standard messaging and "secure" messaging between users. Telegram offers more features than does Signal, but for some tradeoffs in security. Telegram's security is lacking in many ways and only "secure chats" offer end-to-end encryption. Also, the software is not open sourced meaning its security features (such as its encrypted chat protocol) cannot be audited. Oh, and it does require you to link its use with your phone number. But, regardless it is worth mentioning. For more information please visit: https://telegram.org/

Wickr is another secure messaging app that is simply beautiful. Wickr offers "military-grade encryption" and backs its claims through routine third-party audits that can attest to this fact. Wickr also works with hackers by offering "bug bounties" in which hackers who identify vulnerabilities in the software are awarded bounties for their efforts of up to $100,000! Wickr is also open-source and doesn't require you to tie your personal identity to it in order to be used as do Signal and Telegram. Wickr is definitely the best of the three in terms of privacy and anonymity and that is why it is my preferred method of communication. For more information please visit: https://wickr.com

The last method of communication falls into a separate category of its own in my opinion. It is known as Jabber. Jabber is a decentralized instant messaging platform that allows total and complete anonymity for its users. It reminds me a lot of AIM for those of you who remember the 1990s and early 2000s when AOL was in its prime. Jabber allows users to register on independently owned and maintained servers across the globe. Users are then free to communicate with other Jabber users no matter what server they are registered on. Usernames are similar to email address, for example the Jabber username that I use for my company is "OTBTechnologies@jab.im" which was registered with a server in Switzerland. Jabber allows user the ability to utilize what is known as "Off-The-Record Messaging" which provides encryption and plausible deniability to users of this service. Off-The-Record (or OTR for short) is the only way I communicate over this protocol to ensure the privacy of both our my own self and my clients. For more information please visit: https://www.jabber.org/faq.html

File Sharing Methods/Cloud Storage

There are many methods of file sharing over the web, but the best way to stay anonymous and secure when sharing files is to use an encrypted cloud storage provider. Unfortunately, many encrypted cloud storage providers are within the Fourteen Eyes. But, obviously by now you have a good idea of how to stay anonymous enough while online that this should not much so matter.

Moving right along, we will talk about the various major entities that make up the encrypted cloud storage industry at this time.

Starting with the most popular, Mega.nz! This provider is definitely the most popular encrypted cloud storage provider, and they allow users up to 50GB of data to be stored free of charge (if you elect to participate in their "achievements program.") Alternatively, by paying for the service you can have hosted up to 8TB of data. This service can be payed for anonymously using cryptocurrency, and by using other anonymization techniques your use of the service can be completely and totally anonymous as well. Mega.nz uses a concept known as "Zero-Knowledge" so that you can upload literally anything to their servers and since it is encrypted on the user's end they know nothing about the files contents. Mega is open-source and so their encryption protocol is able to be verified by anyone. For more information, please visit: https://Mega.NZ

Another provider that is of interest is Tresorit which is under the jurisdiction of Switzerland. They offer solutions for businesses and individuals for affordable prices. Unfortunately for their cloud storage solutions, they only offer payment via Paypal, Credit/Debit Card, and Bank Transfer. But, there services are top notch so they made it into this guide. Huge plus though, they offer a free service that allows users to send files of up to 5GB for **FREE!** Simply head to https://send.tresorit.com/ using anonymization techniques and upload your file there to get a link to send to the receiving party. All end-to-end encrypted! For more information on their other offerings, please visit. https://Tresorit.com

Last, but not least, is Storj. This one isn't even on the market yet, but when it is released it is going to be a game changer. The way this service works is that your files are encrypted client-side and when they are transmitted for storage the encrypted files are split into pieces and sent to various locations. This splitting of files ensures that your data is not held in one location which would leave the data open to potential attack by an adversary. This company seems likely to offer cryptocurrency as a payment option when they do finally begin offering their service to the public since it fits their business model so well, but only time will tell. For more information of Storj, please visit: https://storj.io/

Verifying the Checksums of Files

Verifying the Checksums of Files is a simple process that is able to prevent catastrophe for end-users of software. SHA256 or SHA512 Checksums should be available for every file you download which you plan to install on your computer. The Checksums serve the purpose of verifying the integrity of the file. Should a file be compromised, there will be a mismatch. Verifying the Checksum of a file is exceptionally easy. All you must do is install an application such as gtkHash and whenever you download a file you plan to open simply have gtkHash generate a Checksum for it. Once, the Checksum has been generated by gtkHash, simply cross reference the generated Checksum with the one provided by the author of the file. As long as these two Checksums match, then you can proceed with opening or installing the file on your computer.

Always make sure that you are obtaining a Checksum from a third-party wherever possible as it would not be difficult for a hacker to alter the Checksum provided by a website that hosts the file if he already has access to the file itself. As you become more familiar with open-source software, anonymity, and cyber security in general these things will make much more sense. In the meanwhile, please check out this resource for more information on verifying Checksums: https://itsfoss.com/checksum-tools-guide-linux/

It is also possible for an individual to use their private PGP key to digitally sign a document that can then be verified through the paired public PGP key. This can be done from the command line in Linux as long as GPG is installed on the OS. To verify that a file has been digitally signed with the trusted party's private key all you must do is obtain the trusted parties public key (in .asc format) and save it in the same folder/directory that contains the file in question. Once that is done, open a terminal and **cd** to the appropriate directory. Once there type **gpg –import [insert trusted party's public key filename here]** and hit Enter to import the signature file. Then, finally, type **gpg –verify [insert trusted party's public key filename here] [insert file in question's filename here]** and hit Enter. Gpg will then display information pertaining to the signed file and whether or not the file was signed using the PGP key

provided.

DD-WRT/OpenWRT Routers

DD-WRT and OpenWRT Routers are examples of routers that have been flashed with custom firmware that support many more functions that their default firmware. While there exists many other custom firmware, these are the two with which I am most familiar. Both DD-WRT and OpenWRT offers a feature known as OpenVPN to allow a user to connect the router directly to a VPN server of their choice and then force all local connections to the router through said VPN connection. OpenVPN Routers are extremely important tools in the quest to become and remain anonymous online. The reason I recommend these routers is because they ensure that all devices connected to them only access the internet through the VPN connection (or the connection to the Tor Network) that they have established. OpenVPN Routers are simply routers equipped with firmware that is designed to allow the user to specify configuration files that instruct the router how to connect to a VPN. All the details on how to set your router up to connect to the VPN can be found on your VPN provider's website.

While it is entirely possible to do, getting a router set up to run through the Tor Network is a more elaborate process. The information required to set a router up to run through the Tor Network is laid out on the Tor Project website here: https://trac.torproject.org/projects/tor/wiki/doc/OpenWRT

By making sure to connect only to the OpenVPN Router that you have configured to route through a VPN, you are making sure that no matter what your internet traffic doesn't accidentally get leaked. This is why I only access the internet through an OpenVPN Router that is connected to a VPN server. When using the applications provided by a VPN provider there is a chance that the connection may drop and, even with the security features many VPN providers offer, there is a chance you may submit sensitive information over an insecure connection that exposes your actual IP. Always use an OpenVPN Router if you truly value your privacy!

TailsOS

TailsOS is an "amnesiac" live operating system that forces all traffic through the Tor Network by default. This operating system is best used in tandem with an OpenVPN Router as it allows the user to access the Tor Network without his/her ISP being any the wiser and it also adds another layer of anonymity to the mix. There is no way to use a VPN with TailsOS outside of this method, but depending on why the user needs the VPN it is suggested that an obfs4 Tor Bridge may be a viable alternative. TailsOS leaves no fingerprint on the device it is used on, and is run entirely from the RAM of the computer. Upon shutting TailsOS down, all data stored in the RAM is erased so there is literally no trace of its having been used.

This operating system can be run as a live USB or live CD depending on the user's needs. If used as a live USB, there is the possibility of using a "persistence" volume to allow the use of foreign programs. This is necessary if the user needs to store PGP-keys or has a desire to use a cold Cryptocurrency wallet for transactions. The use of a persistence volume however opens up the possibility that an adversary could gain valuable information about the user from the data stored there, but so long as the USB drive is kept safe the user has nothing to worry about.

Tails OS is excellent for staying anonymous on the go, but keep in mind that the ISP you connect through will be able to see that Tor is being used thus it is always advised to use an obfs4 Tor Bridge if this is an issue.

Plausible Deniability

This is the perfect opportunity to discuss what is known as "Plausible Deniability." The term was actually coined by the CIA to refer to their protocol for protecting Senior Officials and the President of the United States of America from suffering any repercussions for the illegal programs that were (and still likely are in a covert fashion) being conducted by the Central Intelligence Agency should knowledge of their existence be leaked to the general public. The concept is simple, if the President remains "unaware" of any wrongdoings by this department of the government then he cannot be faulted for doing nothing about their illegal activities. This same concept has been used by many people and organizations outside of the government of course. If something can't be proven beyond a reasonable doubt, then no one can be found guilty in a court of law.

The reason I make mention of plausible deniability is because it is exceptionally useful to those who are at risk of being harshly punished for speaking out in oppressive countries.

Individuals residing in such locations are perfectly capable of using anonymization techniques such as those found in this guide, and if questioned or interrogated they simply have to claim no knowledge of any "wrongdoings." Of course it may be best to err on the side of caution as the judicial systems in such territories is often less than fair, but none the less it is a legal defense worth mentioning.

While the concept of plausible deniability had existed long before the CIA coined the term, its practical application is greater now more than ever before as mass surveillance has become the "new normal." This is the beauty of anonymity; you are truly free to say whatever you want and no one can retaliate against you since they know not who you are! This is why plausible deniability is so important to those who desire to remain anonymous.

If you ever find yourself in a situation where you are being investigated or interrogated in a country that is governed by a totalitarian regime, always remember: Deny, Deny, Deny! No matter what an adversary says or does, Deny! The ultimate goal of those interrogating a subject is to psychologically wear them until their breaking point. Do not cave in to the mind games and you are golden!

Fact vs. Fiction: Hidden Operating Systems

Initially, I intended on writing this section to inform readers about the possibility of using a program known as Veracrypt to create a hidden operating system on a hard drive that would allow for plausible deniability of its existence. This software is well known among those who have done a lot of research on the subject of anonymity and security such as myself. However, there is a common misconception that this program's claims to make the user's hidden operating system appear non-existent to an adversary. After having had more time to thoroughly investigate the subject (as I have done with everything else in this guide,) I have decided instead to write this section to inform readers that Veracrypt has design flaws. While it is a beautiful thought, the plausible deniability factor goes out the window with more thorough research into the inner workings of a hidden operating system. More information can be found in this paper submitted to the ResearchGate website by Dr. Michal Kedziora of Wroclaw University of Science and Technology:

https://www.researchgate.net/publication/318155607_Defeating_Pla usible_Deniability_of_VeraCrypt_Hidden_Operating_Systems

Now, you can still use Veracrypt to create a "hidden" operating system on a device if your adversary is not very technologically advanced or if your adversary regards you as a relatively benign individual and the tactic will more than likely work since they won't bother going to the extremes necessary to detect the presence of a hidden OS. But, just keep in mind that an adversary with more advanced technical know-how and enough motivation will relatively easily be able to detect your hidden operating system through the use of computer forensics software.

File Encryption

File encryption has already been talked about briefly in the previous guide, but not in terms of encrypting files for storage locally. As I spoke of in the previous section, Veracrypt is a very useful program for ultra-high grade encryption. While it is only somewhat useful for creating a plausibly deniable operating system as it claims to be, Veracrypt is extremely useful in encrypting files (or even entire devices; though I personally use LUKS for such things.) Files that are to be transmitted over the internet or is destined to be stored on a server that is not under your total control or one that even has the slightest chance of being compromised should always be encrypted.

Veracrypt allows the user to utilize various ciphers and even allows for the use of cascade ciphering and the implementation of a PIM (Personal Iterations Multiplier.) The cascade ciphering offers the user to use three different encryption algorithms one on top of the next to enhance the level of security offered, and the PIM is defined by the user and determines the number of times the password selected by the user must be hashed in order for the password to allow the encrypted file to be accessed. When attempting to decrypt a file, the person trying to access the file must know both the PIM and the password in order to be successful. These two features provide the user with the highest level of security available in terms of file encryption. It is essentially impossible for an adversary to gain access to a file encrypted in such a way (provided the password used is selected using the techniques covered in the first guide) even if the adversary were to have Quantum Computing capabilities (which have not yet even been fully developed; more on this later in the guide though.)

Veracrypt is able to be used on any operating system, but as you learned in the previous guide Linux is the best OS for security reasons. For more information on Veracrypt, please visit their website: https://www.veracrypt.fr/en/Home.html

Again, some of the claims made by Veracrypt may not be 100% accurate as has been proven by those who took part in the writing of the paper referenced above.

Disk Sanitization and File Shredding

Moving right along, we will now discuss the best methods for disk sanitization and how to shred files so they cannot be recovered using the Linux operating system. These are relatively simplistic tasks that may come in handy for those who are at risk of having their hard drives forensically analyzed by an adversary. Linux distributions typically come with a utility that goes by the name "Disks." This utility is used for, as the name implies, the management of disk drives such as hard drive disks for example.

Something I should mention before we proceed is that this method will only work on traditional magnetic hard drive disks and not flash drives or SSD-type hard drives. Flash drive and SSD-type hard drives are fairly difficult to completely rid of data remenance, but for more information I advise you to check out the NSA's website (yes, you read correctly,) for more information on how to properly deal with such situations:

https://www.nsa.gov/resources/everyone/media-destruction/

I, personally, do not open pdf files on my computer

(especially not ones that are hosted by the NSA seeing as they routinely implement malware to further their agendas) because such pdf files can easily be exploited to infect a users computer with malware/spyware. The Linux operating system is definitely more resilient to such attacks than something such as Windows, but I still refuse to take any chances. If you want to check out the pdf files on the NSA's website I recommend only opening them in a secure environment such as a sandbox or a virtual machine (which we will learn more about later in this guide,) but even then you're taking a bit of a risk.

Anyway, back on track, the Disks utility offers users the ability to overwrite entire devices with zeros which should effectively rid a magnetic hard drive disk of any data remanence. There is a myth that it is necessary to use the "Gutmann-method" which overwrites drives in a specific fashion 35 times in total. This supposedly prevents an adversary from being able to use what is only a theoretically possible ability to forensically analyze the compromised storage media using a magnetic force microscope. Never in history has there ever been a case where this feat has actually been used to gain any useful information from a magnetic hard drive disk, so (as I said) this is only a theoretically possible way to forensically analyze a device. This myth has been circulating for a long time now, but you should know that you are pretty safe doing a single pass wipe with only 0s to sanitize a disk such as that performed by the disk utility. But, if it will help you sleep better at night, you can always do multiple passes using Disks.

Another alternative to using the Disks utility is "Derik's Boot and Nuke" aka "DBAN." DBAN allows users the ability to use several different disk erasure methods (one of which is the Gutmann Method if you insist on using it) to sanitize a hard drive disk. The methods contained in DBAN may be more effective than the Disks utility (which only writes 0s) because it overwrites the entire disk drive with pseudorandom numbers making it more difficult for data recovery programs to decipher useful data from random data written by DBAN. The project (though it is no longer maintained) can be found here: https://sourceforge.net/projects/dban/

And, if you want to be really really sure, you could always

use this handy-dandy product once you're done: https://www.diskstroyer.com (though simply incinerating the hard drive disk is probably the safest option at that rate.)

As far as file shredding is concerned, to securely erase a file on Linux all you have to do is use the **shred** command in the terminal. To use the shred command to securely erase a file, all one must do is change the directory to the one in which the target file is located by using the **cd** command, then execute the **shred** command by typing **shred -xvu -n <number of times to overwrite the file> <filename>** then hitting enter. The terminal will respond by showing you a visualization of what it is doing and then the file will be gone. This command effectively overwrites the individual file with random data then deletes it similarly to how DBAN functions to securely erase entire disks. Again, this method of securely deleting files is only effective on HDD not SDD storage devices.

Proxy Chains

ProxyCap, Proxifier, SocksCap64, and Proxychains all share the same function: they allow users the ability to route the internet traffic of specific applications through a series of proxies (and/or anonymization networks such as Tor.) These programs are pretty self explanatory and each one comes with its own documentation for ease of use.

What you need to know that isn't in these programs' documentation for use is why routing internet traffic through a series of proxies is useful. By routing internet traffic for specific programs through a series of proxies (also known as proxy chains) you are making it increasingly difficult for anyone to trace back your actual identity with every additional proxy you add to the chain.

Black hats often recommend routing traffic through a total of 5 different countries that are outside of the jurisdiction of the Fourteen Eyes. The reasoning given for why to do this is that each country would have to cooperate with one another in order for the investigating party to get a positive ID on the person utilizing the proxy chain. So, by spreading this need for cooperation over 5 jurisdictions (that can be thousands of miles apart) which have no cooperation treaties in place (in terms of intelligence sharing) a hacker is substantially increasing the amount of resources necessary to determine his or her identity.

The principle in place here is that if a black hat hacker makes it so that identifying him or her becomes so taxing on the investigating party (in terms of the resources required) that the investigating party will deplete their resources and give up. Think of it like a game of hide-and-seek on a global scale. Just as in the game of hide and seek, if a person hides well enough, eventually the person "seeking" the person in hiding will get tired and call out, "alle, alle auch sind frei" and the person in hiding will be safe.

To increase the difficulty of identification even further, implementation of tor in the proxy chain can be done as well by running tor on the local host and adding it to the proxy chain as "127.0.0.1:9050" somewhere in the middle of the chain.

If the user so desires, he/she can also set the exit node of the proxy chain to be a proxy in a specific location. This may be necessary if the user needs the traffic to exit in a country that allows access to certain web content that may be censored elsewhere via the internet for example. Traffic routing through exit nodes in certain countries may have content restrictions imposed on them in certain situations. One particular example is in the case of users trying to access particular YouTube content that is blocked based on geoIP in order for YouTube to comply with certain licensing agreements or local laws (though it is technically possible to use this method to circumvent censorship of content, I do not advocate the violation of any laws, local or otherwise; this is just presented for example's sake.) Less commonly, a user may desire to do the same with regard to the entrance node into the proxy chain for varying reasons.

It is very important that you also realize that if one proxy in the proxy chain goes out of service, the connection may fail depending on how it is configured and it may be difficult to identify which proxy it was that died especially if utilizing an exceptionally long chain.

Virtual Machines/Virtualization Software

Virtualization is one of the most incredible things available, not just for the fact that it increases a users ability to stay anonymous and safe online, but also because it allows users the ability to run almost any operating system known to man without actually installing it on their hard drive. This means users can set up a bunch of different Virtual Machines with different profiles so that when they are fingerprinted by online services their identity will appear to be that of the specific machine and not of their host machine. Virtualization software such as VirtualBox can be installed on the Linux operating system to allow the user to run Virtual Machines. Virtual Machines can also allow a user to test out operating systems and software that is not compatible with his host operating system or to open a file that may not be trustworthy in an environment where it is unable to harm the host operating system.

I will not elaborate much further on the topic because I feel I have given you a good idea of what can be accomplished with Virtual Machines, but I highly recommend installing VirtualBox to everyone whether you already plan on using it or not. There will

likely come a point in time where it will be of use to you whether

you realize it now or not. More information on the software can be

found here: https://VirtualBox.org

Whonix

Whonix is an operating system that runs on virtualization software such as VirtualBox that forces all internet traffic to be routed through Tor similarly to Tails OS. By using Whonix you also are able to rest assured that your digital fingerprint is substantially different when using it than when using the host operating system as well since it is a self-contained machine. This also means that the risk of infection by malware is essentially contained only to the virtual machine should anything go awry. Also, the fact that the Whonix Workstation only connects to the internet via the Whonix Gateway which utilizes a self-contained LAN means there is no risk of your real IP being leaked. The Whonix organization has compiled a ton of information on some of the best practices for security and anonymity that you may find useful in addition to that which is found in these guides.

Remember that when using Whonix it is advised that you connect to a VPN whether via an OpenVPN equipped router (recommended) or via software on your device. If you do not, your

ISP will be aware of your Tor usage and you risk the possibility of having your traffic routed through Tor nodes that are operated by an adversary. By using a VPN prior to connecting to the Tor Network you will avoid the possibility that your identity will become known through traffic analysis or direct interception. And, as will be covered in the next section, feel free to add additional hops before or after connecting to the Tor Network so as to increase anonymity if you so please. Whonix is very well designed, but if you do not use it properly it cannot help you.

Whonix is a fantastic operating system that offers a level of security that is hard to beat. For more information on the OS or to download it, please visit the Whonix website at: https://whonix.org

Chaining Anonymization Methods

We already briefly covered this in the section on proxy chains, but I thought I'd make a separate section elaborating on the fact that there are of course other ways to go about chaining anonymization methods. I mentioned in the beginning of this guide that it is ideal to use a router equipped with OpenVPN in order to ensure you are always connected to a VPN no matter what when accessing the internet and this is the best first step one can take. However, one can additionally create a double or even triple VPN (if your VPN provider already offers a "double VPN" option when you connect through their software) by also installing VPN software on your connected device and connecting through it in addition to the VPN to which your router is already connected. This is similar to the concept of chaining proxies, except instead of chaining SOCKS5 Proxies we are chaining VPN servers.

You could alternatively create a series of routers all equipped with OpenVPN/OpenWRT/DD-WRT that are linked to one another in a fashion so that the first router is connected to a

VPN server, the second to the Tor Network, and the third to a different VPN server than the one the first is connected to before the final connection to your device. This is an extremely smart way of going about things because it will route your traffic in a manner that will make it damned near impossible to positively identify as your own as long as all other anonymity techniques covered in this guide are utilized to their fullest potential.

Going a step further, after having yourself set up in such a way with the series of routers, you can then proceed to use a VPN (or double-vpn) connection through the VPN software installed on your device. Maybe even use the Whonix Virtual Machine for a little extra precaution after that even depending on how sensitive of a mission you are conducting. Or perhaps Tails OS is a better option if you fear there is a risk that an adversary may gain physical access to your device.

But, I think you get the picture as far as why one might want to set up a chain of anonymization methods at this point in the reading. Remember though, routing through the Tor Network at any point in the chain will cause your connection to the wider internet to be slower, but much more anonymous of course. And, the more proxies/VPNs/passes through the Tor Network you add to the chain of anonymization methods, the slower your connection will be just the same.

Post-Quantum Cryptography

Post-Quantum Cryptography (also referred to as quantum-resistant cryptography) is called such because it involves the use of algorithms that are though to be resistant to attack by Quantum Computers which are currently being developed. These computers, once fully developed and implemented, will completely change the way that encrypted communications must take place in order to remain secure. Quantum Computers are able to process large amounts of data much more quickly than Classical Computers and thus are able to break codes much more quickly as well. The NIST (National Institute of Standards and Technology) has an ongoing project to encourage the development of Quantum-Resistant Cryptography Standards which will come to replace the current standards as Quantum Computing becomes more prevalent.

Initially, it is thought (reasonably so) that Quantum Computers will be quite expensive so the only adversaries that will be likely to have access to such technologies will be large corporations, criminal empires, and governments. As the technology becomes less costly and the use of Quantum Computers becomes more prevalent the easier it will be for individual hackers and small crime rings to begin using these computers to break previously secure encryption protocols. What this means to you is that it is in your best interest to begin using more sophisticated encryption protocols as they are developed in order to stay ahead of the curve.

To keep this document as concise as possible I will refrain from going into much detail regarding Quantum Cryptography, but if you would like to know more there is a treasure trove of information on the subject that can be found by checking out the following:

Detailed information on Quantum Cryptography and Algorithms that can be used to assure security in a Post-Quantum World: https://blog.trailofbits.com/2018/10/22/a-guide-to-post-quantum-cryptography/

Simple explanation of Quantum Computing and its Effect on Cryptography: https://www.cryptomathic.com/news-events/blog/quantum-computing-and-its-impact-on-cryptography

Another good source with simple explanations of Quantum Computing and its Effect on Cryptograhpy: https://resources.infosecinstitute.com/quantum-computation-and-its-effects-on-cryptography/

Information on a Lattice-Based Quantum-Resistant Encryption Project (written in Java and C programming languages) that can be used in present day to encrypt data/information so that it will remain safe after the wide-spread implementation of Quantum Computers: https://tbuktu.github.io/ntru/

Github for a fork of OpenSSL that uses Quantum-Resistant algorithms: https://github.com/open-quantum-safe/openssl

Github for a fork of OpenSSH that adds Quantum-Resistant Key Exchange and Signature Algorithms: https://github.com/open-quantum-safe/openssh-portable

The official home of The Quantum Resistant Ledger, a Blockchain Technology that is Quantum Resistant: https://TheQRL.org/

Virtual Private Servers

Virtual Private Servers or VPSs for short can be used to work on operations that require the use of a computer connected to the internet aside from that of the user's own. A VPS is simply a virtual machine running on a server that hosts other VPSs as well. VPSs can be used for a wide range of purposes, and just like any other computer can have a wide range of features. Some VPSs have more RAM, better processing power, a more preferred operating system, or more storage than others and access to those with better features accordingly tends to cost more. Typically a user will pay to rent a VPS on a month to month basis. Costs vary depending on provider and some providers allow for users to pay anonymously with cryptocurrency.

Like I said, a VPS can be used for anything you can use your own computer to do, but with a VPS that is paid for anonymously the sky's the limit. I won't elaborate any further on this one; use your imagination. Just remember that many VPSs keep logs (even if they claim they do not) and to always use anonymization no matter what if you truly want to keep your identity a secret.

I might also add that when using a VPS many people opt to use proxy chains as an anonymization method for their activities, but depending on what the intended use for the VPS is the method of anonymization necessary may differ. You're now at a point that I will not elaborate, but instead I ask simply that you use your best judgment.

Antidetect Browser

The Antidetect Browser is an extremely powerful tool for deceiving those who attempt to discover your true identity online. I **highly** recommend only using this browser in combination with the anonymization methods we discussed previously in this guide. If you do not have a solid foundation of knowledge which I attempted to have you build leading up to this point in the reading, you will surely fail in your attempts to effectively use the Antidetect Browser.

Antidetect, as it is most commonly referred to as, is the most sophisticated browser spoofing software available to date. The program has a price tag of $600 for a lifetime license, but it is worth it if you want to have the ability to appear anywhere on the globe you so please while simultaneously having the capability to spoof every detail that your browser provides to websites that it visits. Antidetect is host to tools that allow you to control every detail your browser will transmit about you down to the longitude and latitude coordinates. Known as geo-location spoofing, this is extremely useful if you desire to fool an adversary into believing you are somewhere you are not. This will have them on a wild goose-chase if they are not tech savvy enough to understand what you have done (and many people are not.)

Anti-detect also allows WebRTC spoofing! Most other methods of preventing an adversary access to your IP through WebRTC is through blocking WebRTC altogether which is a dead give-away that you are trying to remain anonymous. There are browser add-ons with some functionality that support WebRTC spoofing, however Antidetect is the cream of the crop. The WebRTC spoofing provided by Antidetect allows you to change the IP your browser transmits to anything you'd like!

Anti-detect even allows you to spoof WebAudio! The WebAudio method of browser fingerprinting is so new that the only adversaries that utilize it at this time are extremely large corporations who make money by extensively tracking users such Google, Youtube, and Facebook for example. The developers of Anti-detect are top notch; I cannot recommend a better browser for remaining anonymous on the web.

Other features boasted by Antidetect include: Canvas spoofing, webGL, font spoofing, Javascript object spoofing, Flash player spoofing, browser headers, and browser language. Additionally, the browser functions client side only which means there is no risk of exposing yourself to the company itself through the use of the program.

This has to be one of the easiest browsers to use since it is based on the Firefox Browser. Antidetect, while being extremely user friendly, is probably overkill in most situations. Though for those who absolutely must keep their identities a secret (say for example a political activist who resides in an extremely hostile territory,) the Antidetect Browser may be a God-send!

Bulletproof/Offshore Hosting

Bulletproof and offshore hosting are often referred to unanimously, but they are not one in the same. A bulletproof host is any web hosting provider that serves data that most other web hosting providers will not. These providers typically do not respond to DMCA take-down requests for example. There are some limitations for things that are immoral and/or illegal in essentially all jurisdictions such as carding activities, botnet operations, child pornography, and other such activities. Offshore hosting on the other hand is, as the name implies, provided by companies whose servers are located offshore. Many offshore hosting companies host content on servers in countries such as Switzerland where freedom of speech is a highly protected right and privacy laws are exceptionally strict.

An offshore host is often used by those hosting content that may be illegal in their own country since the governing laws of the internet are based on the concept that the jurisdiction that is host to the server is the one who's laws apply to the content. So, say for example, you want to host a website that speaks out about the injustices in your country but you reside in a jurisdiction where such statements could result in the imposition of the death penalty. Well, no big deal, one would simply use anonymization and privacy techniques such as those covered in this guide and purchase offshore hosting in a country that permits freedom of speech. Couple that with a little plausible deniability and presto! The content is now able to be accessed by anyone on the internet and the publisher is not in any sort of trouble whatsoever.

Bulletproof and offshore hosting (which, again, are often confused and/or mislabeled) is still sometimes used for nefarious purposes despite claims that such content is not permitted by the hosting service. It is unfortunate, but the way most user agreements are written results in the responsibility falling back on the user so the host cannot be held liable for illegal operations conducted on their servers. So, often times a black hat will operate anonymously and use such services for illegal activities. This is why such services often have a negative connotation especially in developed countries where there is usually little to no need for such as service.

Tor Hidden Service Hosting

Ah, now we are getting to the good stuff! Tor Hidden Service hosting is the hosting of content on "the deep web." As we covered in the previous guides, a specialized browser known as the Tor Browser is utilized to access websites of this type. Hosting can be done both professionally or from home if you are confident enough in your ability to configure your web server in a highly secure fashion. I would recommend that for most people who wish to remain anonymous you use a hosting service as opposed to hosting the content at home. Hosting a completely anonymous Tor Hidden Service requires advanced technical knowledge to a degree that is overwhelming to the average user. As of June 2019, OTB Technologies began offering Tor Hidden Service Hosting.

Additionally, OTB Technologies now offers Tor Hidden Service URL customization at a very low cost as well. The URL customization service allows users to choose the prefix of their Tor Hidden Service. OTB Technologies is capable of providing customization of both legacy (version 2) and the newest (version 3) types of Hidden Service URLs. These prefixes can be generated rapidly by OTB Technologies and can be either 7 or 8 characters depending on your budget and time frame in which you want the URL to become active.

Tor Hidden Services, when configured correctly, make it impossible to discover the owner/host of the website. OTB Technologies allows users to pay via Bitcoin or Monero for added anonymity allowing users to have their content hosted with no ties to their identity. This is one benefit of a Tor Hidden Service, but there are other benefits as well.

Hidden Services are also useful because they allow users of a censored internet to access their content anonymously as well! This means that if your content is not able to be accessed via the clear web in China because it violates their government's standards, but you decide to implement a .Onion website then your content becomes available. That's the beauty of the Tor Network; privacy and anonymity go both ways.

Also, it is worth adding that since all data on the tor network is encrypted that there is no need for the use of SSL when transmitting sensitive data and information. But, as we all know, the deep web is also full of tech savvy criminals so **be careful!** I personally never transmit sensitive data over Tor without using PGP encryption as you never know if your data is going to pass through a malicious Tor node. As long as you are connecting strictly to sites secured with SSL through the Tor network and Tor Hidden Service you should be safe. But, consider the fact that it is already common knowledge among many tech savvy individuals that many governments around the world (including the United States) operate Tor nodes in an effort to monitor the activity of its users. Any site you access that is outside of the Tor Network and does not use SSL will expose you to a potential data breach. Also, it wouldn't be too far fetched to think that a sophisticated adversary may gain access to a server that hosts a Tor Hidden Service which would compromise any data submitted in plain-text. Thus, I will always advise you to encrypt sensitive data using PGP when using the Tor Network. Rule of thumb when operating on the deep web: Trust no one. A Tor Hidden Service that is friendly today may turn into your worst enemy by tomorrow.

I suppose I digressed a little bit in that last paragraph since this is more about you running your own Tor Hidden Service, but none-the-less that information is extremely important for someone who has the intention of utilizing the deep web whether for hosting content or simply accessing it.

Remember, all is fair in love and war; and, some abstract philosophers would like to believe that we are currently experiencing World War III. The main difference between this "World War" and the preceding two is that this war is not being fought on a physical battle field, but rather it is being waged on the web where those with a complex understanding of cryptography and networking protocols have a huge advantage. "One began to hear it said that World War I was the chemists' war, World War II was the physicists' war, World War III (may it never come) will be the mathematicians' war." (*The Mathematical Experience*, Boston: Birkhäuser, 1981.)

Again, please **be careful!** I cannot stress this enough!

Hosting I2P Websites

Hosting an I2P Website, also known as an "Eepsite," is exceptionally easy, but hosting these sites also runs similar risks to hosting Tor Hidden Services in terms of your location/identity being leaked if you are not careful. Simply download and install I2P from https://geti2p.net/en/download then install the program. Once it is up and running, you will see in the router console an icon titled "Free Web Hosting." Click the icon and you will be directed to instructions on how to set up your own Eepsite! Some versions of I2P may have this listed simply as "Website" which will be found under the Local Services category if this is the case. Some other version have it listed as, "Web Server." It seems to change titles every few releases, but all function the same. Of course, there are also other clients that can interface with the I2P network as well. But, in terms of ease of use for hosting eepsites this application is most preferred.

The use of the I2P network is not as popular as that of the actual Tor Network itself, so finding a company that will host an eepsite for you is more difficult. To be honest, I don't even have any leads at this time as there is very little demand in the market right now. Hosting an eepsite from home is still an excellent way to make your content accessible to those who would otherwise be unable to reach it due to internet censorship in their own country.

Monero, Dash, Aeon Verge, Bitcoin Dark and Zcash

Monero, Dash, Aeon, Verge, Bitcoin Dark, and Zcash all have one interesting thing in common: they are untraceable! This is what makes these coins extremely unique and useful when conducting business in an anonymous fashion. Using any of these coins is ideal for transactions that must be highly anonymous and secure for whatever reason. The most widely accepted of the "privacy-coins" is Monero, and you can easily convert your bitcoin to Monero via Shapeshift.

To obtain Monero one just needs to get a Monero wallet at https://MyMonero.com/ or https://www.XMRwallet.com/ and head to https://ShapeShift.io/ to convert your Bitcoin (or other alt-coin such as Litecoin for example's sake) into Monero. Keep in mind shapeshift does log user data such as browser fingerprints and IP addresses.

Might I also add that it would be very wise to create a cold wallet if you plan to hold your monero for any length of time. Reason being is that should either of the two aforementioned websites become compromised, you may well lose access to your funds. A cold wallet ensures that your cryptocurrency is safe and sound.

The best way as of the time of writing to get a cold wallet set up is to head over to https://MoneroAddress.org/ (through a series of proxies/VPN tunnels/tor nodes if you desire maximal anonymity) to generate a wallet address where you can send your monero then physically write down the mnemonic seed for the wallet. After that is finished, it should go without saying that you should send your monero to the address generated and retain the mnemonic seed until you desire to access your funds in the future.

There are more secure ways to store the seed such as PGP-encrypting it and saving it on a server with no traces to you. This would be best if you believe there is any chance that your seed may be at risk of being discovered by an adversary. However, keep in mind this means that your seed would be at risk of disappearing should anything happen to the server. Thus, it is advised to store the encrypted seed in several different locations. Should any of the locations become compromised it would then be advised to repeat the previous steps to re-establish the security of your funds. Of course one could always just store the encrypted seed locally, but that comes with its own set of risks. I'll leave you with this thought: always plan for the worst, but hope for the best no matter how you decide to store your seed.

Crypto-Phones

Crypto-Phones are expensive. I would like to start by making mention of that fact as they are primarily of use to individuals who are part of organizations that must remain anonymous. This isn't to say that individuals couldn't use them, but the other party would have to be utilizing a cryptophone as well in order for the service to be useful. There are many companies offering cryptophones, but I would personally recommend GSMK CryptoPhone since they are the only cryptophone company whose projects are open-source and able to be trust whose products can be seen here: https://www.cryptophone.de/en/support/tech-specs/

Mind you, the high price tag is definitely worth it and will allow you full confidence in knowing that your communications cannot be eavesdropped on no matter where you are on the planet. Traditional phones run the risk of Man-In-The-Middle attacks such as those presented by IMSI catchers which are often utilized by governments seeking to identify terrorist cells, but have now also found their way into criminals' tool kits as well. Peace of mind is definitely worth the money. These phones are especially useful to executives, political activists, and government officials whose communications (when intercepted) could put their entire business in jeopardy, compromise their agendas, and/or endanger their lives.

Anonymous Assets/Shell Companies

Anonymous Assets have been a thing for many decades now as has been made public by the publishing of the "Panama Papers." Shell corporations are corporations that are established anonymously for clients of legal services businesses in countries and jurisdictions where laws permit the formation of a corporation without requiring the corporation's actual owner to be publicly named. This is even possible to do within the United States however there are some who are pushing for lawmakers to change this fact. Once the corporation is formed, the owner of the business can act through the business to open bank accounts and make financial transactions in a relatively anonymous manner. There is no law that prevents citizens of the United States from opening a shell corporation whether at home or abroad.

Shell corporations are still of use since the owner of the corporation can hide his or her assets by having them put in the name of the shell corporation. For example, a car or a house may be put in the name of a shell corporation to avoid having to claim it on a bankruptcy or in a divorce case. The owner of the corporation can then claim that he or she does not own the asset.

There also used to be the possibility of hiding assets in countries where banking privacy laws are more strict such as in Luxembourg and Switzerland, however as of 2010 a law known as FATCA was enacted by the United States which requires all foreign banks to report any dealings with United States citizens (or even those who were simply born in the US or even those who were prior residents) to the United States Department of Treasury. This has resulted in many offshore banks refusing to do business with US clients, and those who do are typically FATCA-compliant. As a result, there has been a huge shift to hiding assets in the form of cryptocurrency as it is exceptionally secure and allows the source of the funds are extremely easy to anonymize. However, if a foreign shell corporation acts as a proxy for a United States citizen then it becomes easy to open an offshore bank account without the United States Department of Treasury being any the wiser.

The Panama Papers exposed the fact that many business people and politicians have been using shell companies for decades to conceal their assets. While this is a method of anonymizing assets that still works very well to this day, I very seldom even make mention of this method of anonymizing assets since many of those wishing to establish such a corporation may have intentions of violating other laws such as those mentioned prior. But, if you would like more information on how to incorporate an anonymous shell company and have pure intentions, please visit: https://Incorporations.io where you can find the best country to incorporate according to your needs. Even if you do not desire to incorporate an anonymous shell company, I do suggest checking out the company's primary website https://FlagTheory.com for some interesting information about becoming an "International Citizen" if you will.

Conclusions

Well, that's it folks! You now know pretty much everything there is to know about becoming and remaining anonymous. There are a few relatively insignificant things that I feel I may have missed such as the alternative social media platform The Diaspora Project, a certain file sharing program known as OnionShare, and the discussion of using IRC anonymously as a means of communication (though a somewhat outdated means of communication.) But, these are things I will cover more in-depth in later editions of this book. For now you have all the extremely necessary information that you will need to comfortably become and maintain an anonymous presence on the world wide web. Now, with a little practice, you will be able to carry out your life in a manner that is consistent with the law yet allows you greater freedom than most people realize they have under the law.

Nothing can stop you now! You're free!

Legal Disclaimer